The Church and the Nicaraguan Revolution

Cesar Jerez SJ

First published 1984 by the
Catholic Institute for International Relations,
22 Coleman Fields, London N1 7AF
in association with:
    the Canadian Catholic Organisation for Development and Peace,
    3028 Danforth Avenue, Toronto, Ontario, and
    Trócaire, 169 Booterstown Avenue, Co. Dublin, Ireland.

The text is based on a lecture given at the Woodstock Theological
Center, Georgetown University, Washington DC, in April 1984.

ISBN 0 946848 50 5

Design by Jan Brown Designs
Printed by the Russell Press Ltd, Bertrand Russell House, Gamble St,
Nottingham NG7 4ET

Historical Background

Nicaragua's revolution received the backing of the churches, especially the Catholic Church. With its priest-ministers and high ranking officials known as Catholic activists, the Sandinista government at times appeared to have a definite Christian complexion. Before the revolution, the Roman Catholic primate, Archbishop Obando y Bravo, had progressively distanced himself from the Somoza dictatorship. He mediated successfully between the Sandinistas and Somoza when the Sandinistas took influential 'Somocistas' as hostages in 1974 and 1978; in January 1977 a pastoral letter from the bishops' conference described the situation in the rural areas as a state of terror; in June 1979 the Archbishop spoke openly of a 'just war', saying that all peaceful avenues had been exhausted. In November 1979, four months after the overthrow of Somoza, in a pastoral letter warmly supportive of the revolutionary government, the bishops said, 'We are confident that our revolutionary process will be something original, creative, truly Nicaraguan and in no sense imitative. For what we, together with most Nicaraguans, seek is a process that will result in a society completely and truly Nicaraguan, one that is not capitalist nor dependent nor totalitarian.'

The Sandinistas had the support of many priests and nuns, who, working in the shanty-towns and rural areas, had first-hand experience of Somoza's greed and brutality. One, Father Gaspar Garcia Laviana, died fighting with the Sandinistas. Three priests accepted ministerial posts in the new government: the Maryknoll Father Miguel D'Escoto as Minister of Foreign Affairs, Father Ernesto Cardenal as Minister of Culture and Father Edgardo Parrales as Minister of Social Welfare. There were also a handful of priests in senior administrative positions.

3

The panorama six years later is very different. The majority of the bishops, at the prompting of Archbishop Obando y Bravo, have withdrawn their support from the revolution; they have campaigned to remove the priest-ministers from their posts and have publicly criticised the Sandinista leadership for their handling of the crisis among the Miskito communities on the Atlantic Coast. They have repeated accusations that the education programmes of the government are really political indoctrination and have expressed fears about atheism and totalitarian rule. They have come to regard the Christian base communities as Sandinista infiltration in the church and have replied by trying to reassert the traditional authority of the bishops. On 29 June 1982 the Pope wrote them a lengthy letter, upholding the bishops' authority, criticising the 'popular church' but at the same time urging the bishops to be more understanding. .

The Pope used his visit to Nicaragua in March 1983 to repeat the message in his letter. The hundreds of thousands of Nicaraguans, the majority of them Sandinista supporters, who squeezed into Managua's Victory Plaza, had hoped for a different message, one of recognition of the suffering of the people, comfort for the bereaved and signs of peace. In their disappointment they heckled the Pope, adding a further element of tension to relations between the Sandinista Front and the Vatican.

Archbishop Obando y Bravo — made a cardinal in April 1985 — has become a focus for members of the conservative opposition who threw in their lot with the Sandinistas when they failed to dislodge Somoza from power through negotiation, but who within months of the Sandinista victory became increasingly bitter critics of the new government which they were unable to control.

The measures taken by the Bishops' Conference to distance the Catholic Church from the Sandinistas have caused confusion and resentment among ordinary Catholics. The poor, who are the beneficiaries of the revolution, cannot understand this hostility. For most of the bishops, and for many middle-class Nicaraguans, however, the people, enrolled in mass organisations, unions, neighbourhood communities and the militia, are a new and frightening phenomenon. No longer are they the hapless victims of repression, exploitation and poverty, seeking the succour of the church, but an organised social class wielding considerable power.

Relations between the Sandinistas and the bishops deteriorated even further when, at the beginning of September 1983, the bishops denounced the new conscription law — 'the law of patriotic military service' — interpreting it as an attempt to mould conscripts to the Sandinista ideology. The Sandinistas, however, want at all costs to avoid an open break with the church and have sought dialogue with both the Nicaraguan bishops and the Vatican.

4

There was further deterioration in 1984. The armed counter-revolutionary groups, the 'contras', turned their attention to economic targets and received the active cooperation of the CIA in mining Nicaragua's ports. The outrage of the US Congress, and the finding of the Court of International Justice in The Hague that the US government was in breach of international law, provided support for the Nicaraguan government's claims that Nicaragua was the victim of international aggression rather than a domestic insurgency.

In this context a new pastoral letter published in April 1984 and signed by all the Nicaraguan bishops, came as a new blow to church-state relations. It called for dialogue with the opposition, including the armed 'contra' groups, making no recognition of their declared aim of overthrowing the Nicaraguan revolution or the lives lost (almost 7,000 since 1980) and the economic havoc which their incursions have caused. This in turn provoked an ill-judged campaign against the bishops in the Sandinista press. The Jesuits, Dominicans and Franciscans in Nicaragua all published statements criticising the pastoral letter and regretting the deepening divisions within the Nicaraguan church.

In July 1984 Fr Fernando Cardenal SJ, then head of the Sandinista youth movement, accepted the post of minister of education. In November he was expelled from the Society of Jesus after refusing to resign his ministerial post. Fr Cardenal had put forward a formal objection in conscience to abandoning a post in which he was serving the people. In January 1985 he, together with Frs Miguel d'Escoto and Ernesto Cardenal, were suspended by the Nicaraguan bishops from the exercise of their priestly functions.

CIIR
April 1985

5

The Church and the Nicaraguan Revolution

Cesar Jerez SJ

Introduction

Central America has undoubtedly achieved a prominence hardly foreseen six or seven years ago. The Vatican shows a lively interest in the events of this region. The present US administration follows closely what happens in the area. The recent Kissinger Report reflects that new-found importance. At the Latin American level, the Contadora group represents an unprecedented, serious and independent-minded attempt at attaining a negotiated peace in a region so hard hit by civil wars. Even if, of late, the sad events in Lebanon have diverted world attention from the region, the temperature of the North-South conflict can still be gauged by Central America. To a lesser extent Central America is also a measure of the temperature changes in the East-West conflict.

The Catholic Church, traditionally an influential social force in the region, is playing an important role in the situation. Most people ask about the role of the Catholic Church in Central America, and at the same time have a superficial opinion about it. This essay deliberately treats the church in isolation from the very complex Central American context, which inevitably entails some simplification.

After a military dictatorship lasting more than 40 years the Sandinista Front for National Liberation took power in Nicaragua, the culmination of a prolonged guerrilla war, which ended in a popular insurrection. In the five years since 1979 the new Nicaraguan government has set a revolution in motion. This government has begun a profound transformation of Nicaraguan life. This revolution has radically changed the traditional structures of land tenure, the educational system, the distribution of national income, the earnings structure, the network of associations — both private enterprise and the labour organisations — the financial system, the organisation of foreign trade, the social impact of the poor majority of the population, etc. Upon this transformation of Nicaraguan society the various 'Marxisms', their theories and practices, have had an influence. The most important role in this process of guided social change has, however, been played by the experiences of national history.

The revolutionary process, in attempting to transform social reality in Nicaragua, has cut through the structures of the social fabric, causing, as one might expect, a profound polarisation among all kinds of social groups, urban and rural associations, religious communities, and the churches, including the Catholic Church. In such a situation, detached discussion is by no means easy. Some of the problems are themselves caused by polarisation: for the actors who play a role in this story, whose personal and economic interests are at stake, the problems of Nicaragua are issues of life and death, or at least are perceived as such.

The topic could be approached by way of a long survey of particular incidents which have provoked conflict, out of which general conclusions of presumably universal value could be drawn. This approach is not adopted here, for several reasons. It could lead us to the enumeration and analysis of a series of events which, even if some of them were felt to be relevant, could also end up as yet another source of either confusion or polarisation, since there are many divergent interpretations of those very facts. In the anecdotal approach, the catalogue of events and persons could become so inexhaustible as to divert attention from the focal point of the problems. It is easy to be carried away by some particular painful fact, by one or another error, by some of the many important documents, by the course of events during the Holy Father's visit to Nicaragua, by the study of the case of Bishop Schlaeffer, by the question of the Miskito people, and so on. The cast list could be endless. This analysis of Church-State relations in Nicaragua will be conducted in a less anecdotal manner, in the hope that this alternative approach will lead to a better understanding of the situation.

The analysis offered here however is made from a *practical theological perspective*. It will not deal specifically with juridical, political, economic or social aspects of the matter except insofar as they underline this perspective.

The church and the central problem of justice and injustice

By now it should no longer be necessary to dwell on the extent of the structural injustice which has ravaged Nicaragua. To transform the structures which caused that injustice is the central task both in Nicaragua and in the rest of Central America. It is true that in the Nicaraguan case pitiless injustice was sometimes alleviated by paternalistic generosity motivated by important religious and humanitarian sentiments, but in spite of such feelings, economic power was still concentrated in a few hands. This is revealed by the statistics of land ownership, always the most important index of wealth and poverty in Central America: in 1979, 2 per cent of the Nicaraguan families owned 46.6 per cent of the land as big landed estates, whereas the bottom 43 per cent of Nicaraguan families had to scratch a living from the land in tiny sub-family-size portions. Before the revolution, illiteracy was the lot of well over 50 per cent of the Nicaraguan population. The elite in Nicaragua used to live in the same luxurious way as in the rest of Central America. Except for some nuances, Chapter III of the recent Kissinger Report represents well this underdevelopment and poverty. This description, superficial and incomplete as it is, should still help to underline what is already well known: the framework of injustice which both accentuates the conflicts inside the church and, at the same time, is a key to understanding the conflicts between church and state.

The understanding of the church underlying this analysis is the one expressed in Chapter II of *Lumen Gentium,* the Second Vatican Council's dogmatic constitution on the church. 'The church' here means the church, and more precisely the Catholic Church, as it is shaped by its hierarchy, its clergy, religious women and men and the laity, the whole people of God.

The profound changes advocated by Vatican II in both the understanding of the inner constitution of the church and the relationship between church and society did not come about all of a sudden. Nor was this true of the re-creation of Vatican II in Latin America both in Medellin (1968) and in Puebla (1979). All these movements of renewal had their forerunners. The Nicaraguan church advocated such changes, even if many parts of this church have been frequently ineffective when the time came to implement them. Many difficulties emerged when the changes which had been called for started to take shape in the church. One must look at these difficulties in order to understand the origins of the different movements in the church. The growth and development of these movements and currents has created an ecclesial unity in which conflict is an intrinsic element. Nevertheless there is no basis for interpreting this conflict as

9

a fundamental division of the church either in faith or in communion.

Unity or division in the church is usually measured against doctrinal or disciplinary criteria. There are no serious divisions in the Nicaraguan church at either level, despite the intolerance of some voices which try again and again to present legitimate theological or practical differences as fundamental divisions. Conflicts, on the other hand, do appear when it comes to different ways of considering the social role of the church inside society, especially as an institution. Conflict is also expressed in the divergent judgments passed by various sectors of the Nicaraguan church upon the value of the competing social models that are engaged today in trying to shape Nicaraguan society. This in itself leads to differences in understanding and implementing the prophetic side of the church's mission. Finally, there is also a significant conflict of spiritualities. Whatever the view various sectors of the church might hold about the nature of the political developments in Nicaragua, alternative religious options are always possible: there can be emphasis on fear or on hope, on leaven-like engagement in the process or on critical self-marginalisation from it, on condemnation or on dialogue.

The newness of what is happening in Nicaragua and the willingness or refusal to give it a chance perhaps bring out the differences between these two religious attitudes. The roots of the tension within the Nicaraguan church have three levels: that of the church's institutional role in society; the church's value judgements on social processes; and the church's religious reactions to these value judgements. This analysis will concentrate on the second level, the value judgements the church makes on social processes and the practical use of the church's prophetic mission in relation to those processes.

Intransigent opponents of the process

A sizeable part of the church, even if it sincerely desires true social change, reacts very strongly when it notices that the groups intent upon that social change — and in the Nicaraguan case that means the revolutionary Sandinistas — make use of Marxist elements for the achievement of this task. The reaction is usually a kind of trauma, which these people apparently find impossible to surmount. They condemn *Marxism* globally without bothering to distinguish between the wide and the genuine diversity of theoretical and practical forms of Marxism. Neither do they take into consideration the various aspects covered by the word 'Marxism'. What Marxism are they dealing with? Economic, social, political, metaphysical Marxism? Nobody in this first group takes such distinctions seriously. Much less do they care about geographical and/or geopolitical analyses of different forms of Marxism.

Their condemnation covers once and for all every one of these very complex aspects and differences. It covers them all under one simplistic label, communism. As a result, their condemnation is total and merciless. It has the traits of a visceral reaction. This position could be summed up as *Anything but communism.* Anything, of course, because communism is intrinsically evil, it is atheistic and it leads to class struggle. By defining 'communism' in this way they can treat it as evil incarnate. In order to root out secular injustice, they cannot tolerate, much less invoke, a system that, though apparently looking for just solutions, would, they believe, bring about consequences even worse than the injustice it tries to eradicate. One cannot be soft with movements which in one way or another unleash the forces that result in communism. John XXIII wrote wisely and audaciously in *Pacem in Terris* that human errors never take away human dignity (para 158) and that philosophical theories must be distinguished from economic, social, cultural or political movements, even if they were given birth by, and took impulse from, those theories because people and social currents are subject to continuous change, personal or historical, and can even faithfully reflect just human aspirations (para 159). The Pope, therefore, concluded that practical contacts with those people or those movements, which had been until recently considered a waste of time, could actually be profitable or become so in the future (para 160). Naturally these important nuances of John XXIII's are in their turn a waste of time for those who brand Marxists and Marxist social movements as absolutely evil. In the face of that evil, resistance must be absolute, even to the point of persecution and martyrdom.

This black and white treatment of the Nicaraguan situation has become the position held by people very high in the hierarchical structure of the Catholic Church. In Nicaragua a noticeable result of this effort has been that few church leaders still have the courage needed to say anything good about the revolution. This shows how much ideology can distort reality. This intransigent position becomes a holy war. In Nicaragua there are some bishops among those who hold this position, either consciously or unconsciously. Historical experience, however, teaches us that intransigence and intolerance have not been good counsellors in difficult and uncertain times. Underlying the church intransigence in Nicaragua is the conviction that the Sandinistas can and must be overthrown. Driven by intolerance, the holders of this view become unable to understand how incorrect it is politically, and — what is sadder — they ignore the cost in human lives lost and in the destruction of Nicaraguan resources for life, and most important of all they disregard the will of the people.

Those in the Nicaraguan church who condemn the revolutionary

11

process as 'communist' emphasise that current communist regimes have always become very hostile towards the church. Some of them see that hostility already present in Nicaragua, and the church already persecuted. Others point out that the Sandinistas are not yet consolidated in power, but they consider that as soon as this consolidation takes place, persecution of the church by the state will inevitably become a fact. Such people constantly remind us that the National Directorate of the Sandinista Front has called itself Marxist-Leninist, inferring that it must be intent on open and direct confrontation with the church. The Sandinistas, they say, do not yet dare openly to persecute the church because the majority of the Nicaraguan people, who are religious, would not tolerate it. So, for the moment, the Sandinistas wait patiently, trying to infiltrate the church, to indoctrinate young people, and to mask their real aims under the cover of dialogue. For this part of the Nicaraguan church the strategy of the 'Sandino-communist' state is crystal clear. Hence the inevitable confrontation. One can even expect that the present formula for holding elections in 1984 will be considered by some church people in Nicaragua as plainly insufficient (as the President of the Bishops' Conference has already said). No benefit of the doubt will be granted. Inside this part of the Nicaraguan church there is to be found a small but powerful sub-segment, linked clearly to movements of the extreme right. These movements are of a political nature, and in other countries of Central America they have become connected with the infamous 'death squads'.

Supporters of a 'third way'

There is another part of the Nicaraguan church, the position of which is characterised, in my opinion, by the following phrase: *'Neither this nor the other solution'*, neither the present awful situation nor any other resembling Marxism. Naturally they oppose age-old injustice and will not accept it for the sake of preventing Marxism. On the contrary, they proclaim the need to fight against injustice, insisting, however, that the establishment of a Marxist regime will bring about more evil than good. They adhere to the 'preferential option for the poor' lifted as a banner by the Latin American bishops in Puebla, but they consider anti-Christian any system that leads to hate or class struggle. They share the position outlined above, that any kind of Marxism is almost inevitably prone to hate and class struggle, but for them this does not justify the defence of the present injustice as a lesser evil. The most difficult problem for this group is to find an authentic way out of this dilemma.

12

In the Nicaraguan case, this group clearly states that they do not want a return to Somoza's system; they do not accept a crude capitalism with excessive dependence on the United States, but neither do they accept the Sandinista regime. At the Central American level, this group has tended to make global condemnation of 'violence from whatever source'. Such a statement might have value, if it were accompanied by active non-violence. The trouble is that it generally does not attempt to reveal or understand the structures and processes that generate such violence. This group often denounces leftist violence with more rigour than rightist or structural violence. In Nicaragua, there has never been an official statement of the Bishops' Conference condemning counter-revolutionary violence and its support by 'covert' US operations.

The defenders of this position in the church feel at ease whenever they have to face up to the injustices of an established regime. In situations like these they pronounce a Christian word of denunciation. They certainly advocate justice, freedom, brotherhood, democracy. This is not insignificant. The problem for them arises when structurally unjust regimes are challenged by revolutionary movements, which are also suspect from this church perspective. But people ask for practical means to put flesh on the bones of their proclaimed 'third way', and in particular for concrete social and political forces capable of implementing this 'third way'. People need politically viable choices and not only moral ideals. Can advocates of the third way state clearly how their values are to be attained by people in Nicaragua today?

A Christian presence in the revolution

Another part of the Nicaraguan church, an authentic part of the people of God, holds the position that a Christian presence within the revolutionary process is possible. They think that the people of God in Nicaragua have won the right to that presence through the great contribution, in quantity and quality, that Christians made to the revolutionary struggle and are making to the revolutionary process. The way they conceive the role of the church could be summed up as follows: *'It is worth the risks involved in order to evangelise the new Nicaragua.'* They do not overlook the Marxist elements involved in building the new Nicaragua. Such elements, however, do not mean that the Sandinistas are pursuing a rigid Marxist strategy to establish a socialist regime. They think that the Sandinistas pay much more attention to national history than to doctrinal Marxism. For them Nicaragua is a crucial crossroads, and is perhaps even beginning to achieve something new and significant for other Third World countries. They do not see the Sandinistas as systematically hostile to the religion of the majority of Nicaraguan society or to the church. They are willing to risk being a critical presence inside the revolution.

This group see the church as the active presence of the leaven; they believe it possible to act as light and salt, according to the gospel's mandate, in the new Nicaragua. They also believe that they must criticise from within the revolutionary process and, if necessary, denounce in the spirit of the gospel the mistakes made by the revolution, and at the same time try to contribute to their correction.

That approach does not confine itself to good intentions. Of course it is not stated easily, much less put into practice, especially when critical support must be given from inside the very structures of power.

This hopeful group, present as well in other countries of Central America, used to call itself 'the church born of the people' or 'the popular church'. They have ceased to use this name both because of misgivings on the part of the church authorities about its possible ambiguity and because right-wing groups in the church have used the phrase with strong emotional overtones. In fact, the right-wing groups, both political and ecclesiastical, speak and write about the popular church in order to misrepresent these groups, and insist upon calling them 'the popular church' so as to have an easier target to attack. Distancing themselves from all such groups, the ultraconservatives try to present themselves as the only faithful church.

On the other hand, people who actually subscribe to a view of the church as 'the church of the poor' by no means want a church without hierarchy. They know rather that there are in the church different functions and charisms, among them the charism of pastors and guides. But, since their vision of the church in society is not that of a powerful institution whose partner would often be the state, they clearly underline the nature of the church as the people of God, whose first citizens are the poor. The structures of this church include not only discipline and obedience, but above all a listening to the Word and an obedience to the Spirit which is reflected in an adult charismatic and prophetic ecclesial community.

It is true, however, that within this part of the church there is also a faction which has made mistakes of the kind denounced by the church members belonging to the first group. These are not so much the priests who, temporarily or permanently, have undertaken delicate tasks in politics proper. These few cases should be treated as exceptions, borderline cases, to be addressed in terms of moral theology and canon law. The problem is rather instances of blind submission to political plans or directives and dubious identifications between revolutionary processes and the kingdom of God. These practical mistakes have sometimes blurred the uniqueness of the church's mission and the ecclesial identity of some of its members. However, a phenomenon which is infrequent, and certainly not deliberately or theologically sustained, has been irresponsibly exaggerated by blanket allegations against this whole part of the church. 'Politicised', 'manipulated by the Sandinista Front', 'church groups infiltrated by Marxists', 'more obedient to the Sandinista *comandantes* than to the bishops', 'useful simpletons': these are only some of the labels attached to those who try to stand fast by the church of the poor. In the present situation of polarisation the attacks, not merely on that possibly misled faction, but also on that whole part of the church, have reached unparalleled levels of viciousness. The right goes so far as to accuse them of heresy.

In times of tension especially, international propaganda and internal confrontation set our first faction, 'the intransigent opponents of the process', against the over-ardent church groups who support the revolution. Often careless or impassioned analyses have as a goal the fostering of hostility between the first and third sectors of the church. The more damaging ideological goal is to push the second sector to side with the first one.

Attitudes to the church within the Sandinista institutions

So far we have outlined the 'dilemmas' from inside the church. We made no attempt to ignore or blur the painful fact of conflict. We come now to the view from the other side of the conflict. That means the question: what is the Sandinista attitude toward religion and the church? How is this attitude translated into political and ideological practice?

The official statement on religion and the church of the National Directorate of the Sandinista Front, issued in October of 1980, is quite detailed and far-reaching. At that time, the secretariat of the Front addressed an official letter to all members explaining that the position expounded by the document was politically binding on all the members of the party. The statement on relations between church and state was ratified on at least two subsequent occasions, one of them at the end of the papal journey to Central America, which in Nicaragua had so tragic a character. No honest observer of the Nicaraguan situation can conclude that the stated Sandinista position is not serious.

The statement in itself is historic. It is the first declaration of a

Marxist-inspired political movement *in power* that states not only that religion is a right of conscience for every citizen of the state, but also that in recent Nicaraguan history Christian faith has shown itself to be an active force for justice even at the level of the institutional churches. In this historic judgment the document expressly contradicts those theoretical statements of traditional Marxism which dismiss all religious beliefs as always delusory and reactionary.

Of course a statement is only a statement and much hangs upon its official political and practical implementation. Therefore it is useful to examine closely the Sandinista practice with regard to religion and the churches.

Let us proceed again by way of a typology. There are in the Sandinista Front people who firmly adhere to the dogmatic Marxist-Leninist interpretation of religion, both theoretically and practically. These people believe precisely what the Sandinista Front denies, namely that religion is always delusory and reactionary. They include people who nonetheless adhere to party discipline and keep their beliefs to themselves. Others possibly do act, at least sometimes, according to their beliefs. When they do so, conflicts with religious people and the church are inevitable. But this doctrinaire group seems to be in the minority in the party. They certainly do not have the upper hand in the Sandinista National Directorate, which in this matter of religion, as well as in other usually controversial areas among so-called Marxist revolutionaries, tends to support a middle course of mixed economy, political pluralism, and non-alignment.

There are other people who adhere in principle to the orthodox Marxist theses. They believe, however, that it is pointless to struggle against religion, and hence against the churches. They think that the development of revolutionary processes with their tendencies towards secularisation will slowly reduce the impact of religion on people's minds. Until a general cultural process leading to the emergence of a scientific and technological attitude has run its course, it would be useless to try to affect the religious sentiments of the people artificially. Thus they normally abstain from confrontation with religion and the churches.

Others, a third type within the Sandinista Front, have had a religious tradition in their families, as has the majority of the Latin American population. However, either because they have become disillusioned with the institutional church or simply because they think that the work of the revolution has the capacity to absorb them, heart and mind, they have, so to speak, put religion and church attendance aside, at least for a while. Other things seem to them to take a priority in this particularly exciting time of their national history.

There is a fourth type, people who keep on being religious and have never ceased to accept the Catholic faith. They are, however, confused, sometimes even estranged from sacramental practice, except perhaps for baptising their children. As Sandinista militants they are firmly convinced the Nicaraguan revolutionary process offers for the first time material and spiritual dignity to the oppressed and impoverished people of the nation. They cannot understand the reticence, much less the attacks, which characterise the attitude to that revolutionary process of many clergy in the Catholic Church. Their reaction is manifested in abstention from sacramental practice and from church groups.

Finally there are also people affiliated to the Sandinista Front who keep alive a fervent faith and reaffirm their resilient hope by a firm decision to participate in every aspect of church life. Their Christian and revolutionary beliefs are expressed in their conviction that there is no contradiction between being Christians, active members of the people of God, and being Sandinista revolutionaries. It is precisely this group whom other members of the church accuse violently of being a fifth column of Marxism within the church. Their position is not easy to maintain, because they certainly do not enjoy the pastoral sympathies of many of the clergy in authority. However, they feel consoled by firmly adhering to what they believe to be Jesus Christ's mandate: 'You are the light of the world, you are the salt of the earth'. Their witnessing Christian presence in the heart of a revolutionary process in power is almost unique and has shaken the conventional wisdom of orthodox Marxist revolutionaries in Latin America and in Europe. This group is not limited to the well known (and very few) priests, who, as noted above, are exceptional cases. It consists of laywomen and men, of all ages, from both poor and well-to-do backgrounds. Some of them have come together in specific church communities precisely to deepen their faith.

This is the spectrum of tendencies with regard to religion and church inside the Sandinista Front. It would be too speculative to venture numbers or percentages, but the majority is probably spread among the second, third and fourth types. This is the reason why in Nicaragua today there are many instances of confrontation between church and revolutionary institutions, and yet up to now there has been a constant search for dialogue. The more profound explanation for this is the respect of the revolutionary institutions, generally speaking, for the Catholic awareness and affiliation of the great majority of people. This could be due exclusively to political realism. On the other hand, there is the fact that very religious people are genuine partners with the leaders in the construction of the revolutionary institutions. This of course says something for caution and sophistication when the Sandinista leaders have to make decisions which touch on the religious character and church affiliation of the Nicaraguan people.

Areas of particular conflict

In Nicaragua's social and political life there are areas in which conflict between church and state or the tensions within the church are experienced with special intensity. Of course, they cannot be isolated from each other since they are often related.

Religion itself. Religion in Nicaragua is everybody's concern. In a certain way in Nicaragua today everything pervades religion and religion pervades everything. It is similar to the mood in the city of Puebla in 1979 at the time of the third conference of the Latin American Catholic bishops, when newspapers carried headlines on the influence of the conference's documents upon almost every aspect of Latin American life, and when people even marched through the streets of the city to demonstrate for or against the theology of liberation, as if the times of the Councils of Nicaea and Ephesus were among us again. This of course demonstrates the relevance of religion in Latin America today. But the other side of the coin is the frequency with which people of very diverse political interests try to manipulate or ideologise religion. When political and social matters are dealt with *indiscriminately* in the name of God, it is difficult to control passions and achieve serenity around issues. In the final analysis every political position seeks a word of support from the church.

The discipline of the church. Church discipline now reflects the tensions within the church or conflicts between church and state. Disciplinary measures have been taken against priests or religious women who, in some bishops' view, are more faithful to Sandinism than to catholicism. Jurisdiction is given or taken away, religious houses receive canonical permission or not, parishes are given or taken away from priests. Often these actions are based upon criteria in which pastoral and political matters are confused. One of the thorniest problems is the vagueness with which some bishops define what is and what is not pastoral work. Religious orders working in higher education or in research often have trouble of this sort: they are not considered to be doing apostolic work.

On the other hand, the mass popular organisations frequently raise their voices or even demonstrate publicly in favour of those priests or religious whom they consider either discriminated against or threatened with disciplinary measures. This kind of impassioned participation by organised people has resulted in accusations that the state is manipulating the situation or introducing 'unruly crowds' into the affairs of the church. Every new incident is also covered widely by the international press and is used to attack the revolutionary process. These street demonstrations have been portrayed as signs of persecution against the church. Curiously enough, every one of these events soon passes into oblivion, mainly because of the inconsistency of the grounds upon which it was fabricated, and one waits for the next episode in the serial. Of course some of the incidents arise out of real mistakes on the part of the mass organisations, but more frequently, however, it must be said that there are abuses of church authority and a certain lack of proportion between the real and the symbolic importance of these events.

This is the context of another continuing problem, the matter of the priests in public office or in party organisations. Clearly the law of the church forbids priests to take up those responsibilities (cf. CIC 285-287), allowing for only very specific exceptions. It is also obvious that Pope John Paul II does not want the priests to stay in their posts. On the other hand, the Nicaraguan government thinks that, after three special missions sent to the Vatican, this matter has been negotiated and has to be regarded as settled at least as long as the Nicaraguan state of emergency lasts. Since this state of emergency is not regarded by the government as only a matter of law but also as a matter of real national emergency, and since the definition of emergency has not been agreed upon, the whole business continues to be a subject of dispute. Attempts by church authority to equate the new church canon law with church practice could revive the conflict once again.

The mishandling of disciplinary matters has caused a deterioriation in the authority of the Nicaraguan church. This deterioriation grows almost every day, especially in some dioceses. Nobody is certain how many in the church submit to rules which they consider arbitrary. The fundamentalist sects, moreover, profit daily from this situation. Because of this, and for purely administrative reasons, the Vatican should intervene as a mediator with the goal of restoring healthy relations between the various sectors of the church. Mutual tolerance should become a principle in the Nicaraguan church.

Doctrinal aspects. Some of the issues that introduce conflict into the unity of the Nicaraguan church are of a doctrinal or theological nature. Hardly any of them touch upon matters of dogma, although extremists have an interest in presenting these conflicts as dogmatic. The role of the church hierarchy is a good example: there are those who proclaim an identity between bishop and Jesus Christ without any theological nuance. There are also those who, following this logic, try to claim that bishops' opinions in the autonomous realm of social and political questions are essential parts of the church's faith. Any number of examples could be given to show how the domain of Christian obedience to bishops has been extended. A typical extreme reaction on the other side has been the attempt to minimise the importance of the pastoral role of bishops in the church, or to identify the kingdom of God and the revolutionary process.

Young people are another focus of conflict. Young people are the future of church and country, much more so in Nicaragua and other Latin American countries than elsewhere in the world. More than two-thirds of the population in Nicaragua are less than 24 years of age. In addition, the revolution has been primarily the work of people under 30 and most young people have supported revolutionary tasks and ideals since the victory. The young are in a state of ideological and political ferment. Young people do not always possess adult religious maturity, and the hierarchy's distrust of the revolution is leading to a greater falling off of church participation among young people than among adults, especially in the towns.

The middle and upper classes in Central America have always been extremely sensitive about anything affecting their children. Among these rather thin strata of the Nicaraguan population, there are frequent charges of ideological indoctrination in the field of public education, and fears are expressed that the church will not be able to maintain its system of Catholic education. Neither the repeated statements of respect for Catholic education made by the Ministry of Education nor the freedom which prevails in Catholic schools has been enough to allay those fears. The question of the Cuban advisers in higher education is also a source of conflict. Of course the church has always taken an active part in these educational matters everywhere in the world, and Nicaragua is no exception.

The Patriotic Military Service law — conscription — which was passed last August, is also an issue. According to the majority of the bishops, it would be immoral to require young people to serve in an army which, in their opinion, serves the Sandinista party rather than the nation. For the revolutionary legislators, however, there is a national consensus on the need to transform Nicaraguan society and that need cannot be met without a revolutionary army, as the case of Allende's Chile sadly proves. It is national sovereignty, regained by the poor through revolution, that is at stake. Hence the obligation of military service. Of course the children of the middle and upper classes never had to serve in the army in pre-revolutionary Nicaragua, as they do not have to serve in Guatemala and El Salvador these days. Some of them have already left Nicaragua, gripped by a very dubious panic. In Central America all the armed forces, with the exception of officers, have always been made up of poor peasants, and it was only among them that the obligation of military service was enforced.

The security of the state. The security of the state has developed into another field of conflict. In a war situation, aggravated by an economic blockade and the distortions of propaganda, US 'covert' operations and counter-revolutionary attacks continue, causing the deaths of many Nicaraguans (almost 1,000 in 1983) and considerable destruction of the productive infrastructure of the country. The security service tries to prevent the development of internal fronts or fifth columns. This is why some foreign priests' residence permits have been cancelled. The procedure has been to hand these priests over to their countries' embassies and to cancel their permits after accusing them of conspiring with the counter-revolutionaries or of inciting people to act against the government.

The response of the church has been to accuse the state of persecuting the church and to criticise other sectors of the church either for not defending their fellow Christians against persecution or — still worse — for consenting to act as members of the state security forces against their own brethren. When something like this happens, the tension within the unity of the Nicaraguan church reaches extreme levels. In such situations, few of our intransigent opponents have remained calm enough to remember that in revolutionary Nicargua, as opposed to contemporary El Salvador or Guatemala, no delegates of the word, no catechists, no religious women or men, no priests, no bishops, have been murdered by the government, and that foreign pastoral workers have much less difficulty in getting their residence permits than in El Salvador or Guatemala.

Competition between church and state for lay leaders. Generally speaking, and in some rural dioceses much more than in the predominantly urban ones, the Catholic church has made a great effort to prepare women and men as pastoral leaders. There are catechists, delegates of the word, deacons, leaders of grassroots communities and so forth. Usually they are persons of considerable prestige in their local communities. At the same time the revolutionary popular organisations, the militia battalions, even the Sandinista Front, try to recruit these very respected people for difficult responsibilities and leadership. Pastoral workers, of course, are able to exert Christian influence in those crucial political and civic positions, but their new responsibilities take up most of their time and force them to neglect the direct work of evangelisation. Some parishes, and even some dioceses, experience this as the loss of their best prepared and most generous personnel, even if, from another point of view, it can be argued that the church's pastoral work also gains.

A look towards the future and some recommendations

Faced with the complexity of the situation, an individual attempt to suggest steps towards a solution could seem arrogant. While this essay is motivated by pastoral, not political, concern, some people might argue that the description of the problems given here is itself biased. To give an unbiased description of Nicaragua today is perhaps impossible. What is important is the attempt to approach all the

problems from the perspective of the Gospel, honestly and calmly —
the problems could have been presented here much more dramatically.
Any attempt to address the conflict-ridden unity of the Nicaraguan
church without blind subjectivity is a contribution to easing the
tension. The first step is to analyse what is actually happening.

People have already taken sides. Quiet rigorous analysis is needed
to make possible Christian discernment without which no church
problem can be adequately solved. Realism, some emotional
detachment and Christian love are necessary ingredients to start easing
tensions.

Results of the analysis of the general situation and of each field of
conflict should then be brought to an *open and sincere dialogue* in
which representatives of the poor majority of Nicaraguan Catholics
should be incorporated. At present mutual trust inside the church, and
confidence between one part of the church and the state, are lack-
ing. Without trust and credibility, progress towards solutions is
impossible. We must accept in advance mistakes and mis-
understandings; they should not stand in the way of a profound
desire for mutual understanding and of listening to each other. No
part of the church should be *a priori* excluded from sharing in this
dialogue among sectors of the church, nor should the church or state *a
priori* exclude parts of each other from the dialogue. No party has the
right to disqualify another by the use of emotive labels, which is what
right-wing groups have done in Nicaragua and throughout Latin
America. Christian and human tolerance are indispensable, or the
conflicts will fester and lead to irreparable ruptures. Two aspects of
the problem are particularly worrying, the intransigence of the
Christian right and the growing alienation of young people from the
hierarchy. Finally, to start the dialogue, as well as openness and
sincerity, there must be a generous capacity to forgive and forget. In
this context, the existing trend of class struggle should become not a
fear but rather a challenge for church people. It is not by ignoring that
trend that reconciliation can be attempted, but precisely by
acknowledging it and trying to overcome its causes.

The Nicaraguan church must meet the great challenge of
rediscovering its mission in the revolutionary context. Within this
context the church's task of proclaiming the good news to the people
has not vanished; rather it should shine with brighter light. Out of the
new situation the Christian call to evangelise all the Nicaraguan
people, and mainly the poor, must be heard louder than ever. Faith,
hope and love for the Father of Jesus Christ can be made operative
through an authentic striving for justice. Drawing on past experience
of the universal church, the Nicaraguan church will find ways of
incarnation in the new revolutionary structures of society. Nothing
can be redeemed which avoids incarnation; and in the revolutionary

processes, as in the processes of the church renewal, there is also sin which must be redeemed. For a church gifted with the power of the Spirit this challenge should not be considered a 'mission impossible'.

The Nicaraguan case cannot be isolated from the Central American context nor from an even broader international one. Inside the Catholic church and inside other churches as well, many people and institutions have — thanks to the grace of God — attempted to help the Nicaraguan Catholic church to overcome its present conflicts. They certainly can and will carry on this fraternal task. We are grateful for these contributions and keep counting on them as true solidarity which looks forward to the overcoming of the crisis we are immersed in. Looking at the future with the piercing eyes of hope, I see both in the church and in the revolutionary state commitments to dialogue, the authenticity of which I have no right to doubt. On those commitments Christian solidarity with Nicaragua should be grafted.

The role of outsiders

It is often said that we Latin Americans blame others for our mistakes and problems, and that charge should also be analysed honestly. In the case of Nicaragua, however, outsiders have a role to play — they are already very active. If our country is invaded, if 'covert' operations against the revolution are unleashed ever more aggressively, if distortions of the Nicaraguan situation are carefully cultivated in the images and words of the media, passions in Nicaragua will also keep flaring up. Some people abroad — and in Nicaragua — argue that if 'pressure' (as they call it) upon the Nicaraguan government ceases to be exerted, then the government will become consolidated and more audacious in persecuting the church. This, however, is the most salient example of fanaticism and cynical distortion. The words 'pressure upon the Nicaraguan government' conceal a thousand deaths of Nicaraguan citizens last year, many of them murdered with unspeakable cruelty by former Somoza National Guards, 'covertly' supplied with weapons by the CIA. These events should be a matter of concern and serious reflection for sympathetic outsiders, and particularly for Christians.

On the other hand, if intransigence gives way to tolerance of the independent existence of a revolutionary regime, if aggression is terminated and Nicaragua can at last start to build a new society in peace, understanding within the church and between church and state could also become less painful.

Nicaragua keeps on offering to hold sincere and frank conversations with the US government. When and how wide will the gates of the rich be opened to the poor without humiliating them?

When and how clearly will the voices of the poor be heard by the rich? At present I see no willingness on the part of the United States administration to open an honest and respectful dialogue with Nicaragua. The United States government accuses the Sandinista government of trying to conceal its true Marxist-Leninist nature and thereby denies Nicaragua the right to act as a truly independent nation and the right to be heard honourably. Instead there is an active determination to eliminate revolutionary Nicaragua, to destroy it completely, no matter what the cost.

Adapting the words Archbishop Romero used shortly before his murder, I ask you, I implore you in the name of God, in the name of the Nicaraguan people and church, do everything in your power to end the constant harassment of Nicaragua, to ensure that peace has a chance before destruction becomes irreversible, as in Vietnam. I ask all people of goodwill to facilitate the necessary dialogue, and to throw no more fuel on the fires of hatred and distortion.